How Things Grow

From Seed

to Sunflower

Sally Morgan

Chrysalis Children's Books

First published in the UK in 2002 by
Chrysalis Children's Books
An imprint of Chrysalis Books Group Plc
The Chrysalis Building, Bramley Road,
London W10 6SP

Paperback edition first published in 2005

ISBN 1 84138 373 2 (hb)
ISBN 1 84458 258 2 (pb)

British Library Cataloguing in Publication Data
for this book is available from the British Library.

Series editor: Jean Coppendale
Designer: Angie Allison
Picture researchers: Sally Morgan and Terry Forshaw
Consultant: Bethan Currenti

Printed in China
10 9 8 7 6 5 4 3 2 1

Picture acknowledgements:
All photography Chrysalis Images/Robert Pickett with the exception of:Front cover (main) & 5
Papilio/Sue Bishop; 6, 28 (TL) & front cover (inset) Papilio/ Robert Pickett; 13 Premaphotos Wildlife/Ken
Preston-Mafham; 18 & 28 (BR) Papilio/ Alastair Shay; 21 Ecoscene/Gryniewicz; 23 NHPA/Roger Tidman
25 Ecoscene/Kay Hart; 26 Ecoscene/Andrew Brown; 27 (T) Papilio/Pat Jerrold, (B) Papilio/Ken Wilson.

What is a sunflower?

A sunflower is a type of plant that produces flowers. The tallest sunflowers grow to heights of two metres or more. Most sunflowers produce large yellow flowers in summer.

The sunflower has a shoot above the ground with a flower, leaves and stems. The roots grow under the ground.

Sunflowers can be grown as a crop. Their seeds are rich in oil. Sunflower oil is used in cooking.

The flowers turn into fruits that contain seeds. In the autumn, the seeds fall to the ground. In spring, the seeds start to **sprout** and grow into a new sunflower plant.

5

The seed

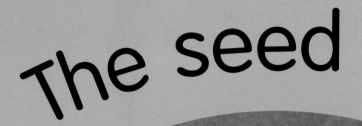

This sunflower seed is about 1 centimetre long.

The life cycle of the sunflower starts with a seed. The seed of the sunflower is shaped like an oval. The outside of the seed is hard and dry. This is called the seed coat. The seed coat protects the tiny **embryo plant** inside.

The embryo plant grows into the new plant. Inside the seed is a food store. The new plant uses the food when it starts to grow.

Inside the seed, is a tiny embryo plant and two seed leaves. The seed leaves are pale brown in colour and filled with food.

Beginning to grow

The seed coat splits and a tiny root appears and grows down into the soil.

The growth of a seed into a seedling is called **germination**. A sunflower seed needs air, warmth and water to germinate.

The shoot grows upwards towards the top of the soil, carrying the two seed leaves.

8

The seed takes up water. It swells in size and this makes the seed coat split. First, a tiny root appears which grows down into the soil. Then a shoot appears.

The seed leaves are small and fat. They contain food which the seedling uses to help it grow.

Leaves and stems

New leaves appear at the top of the stem.

The sunflower grows quickly. After about a week, the shoot is several centimetres tall and the first proper leaves have appeared. The leaves of the sunflower are thin and flat.

The stem is thick and strong. It has to support the weight of all the leaves.

10

The
stem of
the sunflower
is very hairy. This
stops insects landing and
moving over the plant.

The leaves are shaped a bit like a heart.
Each leaf is attached to the main **stem**
by a short stem. The leaves grow in
pairs. There are two leaves opposite
each other on the stem, then a gap,
and then another two leaves.

Growing tall

Sunflowers grow upwards towards the Sun. Most sunflowers are tall plants and grow above other plants. This means they can get plenty of sunlight.

The leaves of the sunflower are held out to get the Sun.

Sunflowers and other plants make their own food in their green leaves and stems. They need light to make their food. They also need a gas from the air and water from the ground.

Sunflowers are such tall plants that they are not shaded by other plants.

Underground roots

The sunflower has a **mass** of roots to hold the plant in place and stop it from being blown over. The roots are long and thin. They are important because they take up water from the soil.

The roots of the sunflower spread through the soil, away from the base of the stem.

Some of the lower leaves on this plant are not getting enough water. They are beginning to wilt.

The water contains **nutrients**, which the plant needs to stay healthy. The water moves up the stem to the leaves. If the roots do not take up enough water the leaves become floppy. This is called **wilting**. If there is no more water, the leaves will **shrivel** up and die.

The flower

The large sunflower is made up of tiny flowers grouped together. There is a ring of bright yellow **petals** around the outside of the flower. The male and female parts of the flower are found towards the middle.

The **flower bud** is made up of green sepals. The sepals cover and protect the petals inside.

The sepals open up, forming a green ring around the flower. Then the petals begin to open.

The flower is fully open. The bobbly bits are the stamens. The carpels are found in the middle of the flower.

The male part of the flower is the **stamen**. Each stamen has an **anther** which produces tiny powdery specks called **pollen**. The female part is called the **carpel**. It is made up of a **stigma**, **style** and **ovary**.

Insect visitors

Many insects visit the flowers of the sunflower. They are attracted by the brightly coloured petals and the **nectar**. As insects crawl over the flower they become covered in pollen.

A field of sunflowers attracts many types of insects including bees and butterflies.

When insects visit other sunflowers, they brush pollen onto the stigmas of the flower. The movement of the pollen from one flower to another flower is called **pollination**. Once pollination has taken place the plant can produce seeds.

Fruits and seeds

Once the flower has been pollinated, it starts to die. The flower head bends over and the petals wither and drop off. As soon as pollination has taken place, the ovaries start to swell up.

The flowers are open for a week or so and then they die. The flower head bends over and the petals drop off.

The flower head is full of swollen fruits. There is a seed inside each fruit.

The ovaries turn into fruits. The plant provides the fruits with lots of food. The seeds develop inside the fruits. The walls of a seed dry out and harden to form a seed coat.

Scattering seeds

In autumn, many birds
visit the dying sunflowers
in search of food.
They land on the
flower head and
pick out all
the seeds.

As the old
flower head
becomes
drier, the
seeds drop out.

Some of the
seeds fall to the
ground and others are
dropped by birds as they
fly away. The seeds stay
in the soil in the winter.

Many
seed-eating
birds such as
finches and tits
feed on the
sunflower seeds.

How long do they live?

Sunflowers are annual plants. This means they live for one year. The seeds germinate in spring. The plants grow quickly in the summer and produce their flowers and seeds by autumn. Then the whole plant dies.

These sunflowers are dying. The leaves and stems have shrivelled and turned brown.

Biennial plants live for two years. They grow through the first year and produce their flowers and seeds in the second year and then they die. Foxgloves are biennials. Perennial plants live for many years.

The ox-eye daisy is a perennial plant that lives for many years.

The sunflower family

This meadow is full of a large daisy called the ox-eye daisy. It has a large white flower with a yellow centre.

The sunflower belongs to the daisy family. This large family includes plants such as the dandelion, thistle and cornflower. Many of these colourful plants are found in gardens and parks. Plants such as dandelions, daisies and thistles are called weeds.

The thistle is a prickly plant with purple coloured flowers.

A weed is a plant which grows where it is not wanted. Weeds grow quickly and produce lots of seeds.

The yellow flowers of the dandelion open in the morning and close again in the afternoon.

The life cycle

1 The seed is protected by a hard coat. Inside is a tiny embryo plant.

2 The seed takes up water and the seed coat splits open. A tiny root appears.

8 The petals fall off and the fruits form. Inside each fruit is a seed.

7 Many insects visit the flower in search of nectar. They pollinate the flower.

3 A shoot appears above ground.

4 The young seedling uses the food in its seed leaves to grow.

6 The flower bud appears at the top of the shoot. It grows larger and then opens.

5 The shoot grows quickly.

Glossary

anther   The male part of the flower that produces pollen.

carpel   The female part of the flower, made up of a stigma, style and ovary.

embryo plant   The young plant inside a seed at its earliest stage of growth.

flower bud   A leaf or flower before it opens.

germination   The growth of a seed into a seedling.

mass   A large number.

nectar   Sweet, sticky liquid produced by flowers to attract insects.

nutrients   Substances that plants and animals need for healthy growth.

ovary   The female part of the flower which becomes a fruit.

petals   The parts of the flower that are often brightly coloured to attract animals.

pollen   Yellow powdery specks that are produced by the anthers.

pollination   The movement of pollen from the anther of one flower to the stigma of another.

sepals   Green flaps, a bit like petals, that protect the bud before the flower opens.

shrivel   To dry up and die.

sprout   To begin to grow.

stamen   The male part of a flower, made up of an anther supported on a stalk.

stem   The main stalk of a plant.

stigma   The tip of the carpel.

style   The part of the carpel that joins the stigma to the ovary.

wilting   Losing support and becoming floppy.

index